FROM
Buddy
TO THE
Beatles

FROM Buddy TO THE Beatles

When the Regent Rocked

STEPHEN FOSTER and DAVID KINDRED

Old Pond
PUBLISHING

Acknowledgments

Many of the photographs in this book were taken by David Kindred when he was working for the *East Anglian Daily Times* and the *Evening Star*. These are reproduced by courtesy of the Archant Group.

The programmes and other memorabilia have been kindly supplied by David Lowe, Stan Singleton, Sandra Warner and Richard Wootton.

Special thanks are also due to Nigel Pickover, Editor of the *Evening Star* and Gerald Main, Editor BBC Radio Suffolk, as well as to Hazel Clover and all their staff at the Regent for their help with this project.

First published 2004
Copyright © Stephen Foster and David Kindred 2004
The moral rights of the authors in this work have been asserted

ISBN 1 903366 65 8

Published by
Old Pond Publishing
Dencora Business Centre, 36 White House Road,
Ipswich IP1 5LT United Kingdom

www.oldpond.com

Cover design and book layout by Liz Whatling
Printed and bound by Butler & Tanner Ltd, Frome and London

Contents

Introduction

REGENT PICTURE HOUSE, IPSWICH.   No 47.

Back in the days when the Regent rocked to legendary acts like Buddy Holly, Eddie Cochran, Gene Vincent, The Everly Brothers, The Beatles and The Rolling Stones the theatre was known as the Gaumont. Most of the rock'n'roll stars from the era this book covers performed at the venue and when Beatlemania swept the nation in 1964 John, Paul, Ringo and George gave the town a night it will never forget.

The Regent has a fascinating history. It began life as a cinema and opened to the public on 4th November 1929. It was designed by architect W. E. Trent of Regent Street, London and was constructed by McLaughlin and Harvey Ltd for Provincial Cinematograph Theatres Ltd. It was very much state of the art boasting 1750 seats, a Wurlitzer organ and a restaurant. At that time it was the new world of cinema calling the shots but the auditorium had also been built to stage theatre productions and concerts, and the building's flexibility was to hold it in good stead.

During the Second World War the Regent played an enormous part in sustaining public morale by providing some much-needed escapism. After the war it continued to enjoy great popularity presenting the Ipswich Civic Concerts, Sadler's Wells Ballet productions and one-night band shows as well as all the latest movies.

Jiving at the Gaumont. A typically full Victor Sylvester Dance Studio ballroom as rock'n'roll reaches Ipswich.

In the 1950s the restaurant was closed down and replaced by The Victor Sylvester Dance Studio. That proved to be an extremely popular move and it's a good bet that many people reading this will have met their wife or husband under the dance hall's glitterball. As rock'n'roll took hold, the Regent, by now known as the Gaumont, was the natural place to meet and to dance to all the music that quickly caught the imagination of the teenagers of the day. The real icing on the cake was to be able to see many of the pop stars in person when top singers and groups came to town heralding an exciting new era of live music.

A key figure in the history of the Regent is David Lowe who managed the theatre from 1958 to 1989. He witnessed first hand the incredible change in popular music. He saw it all from Buddy to the Beatles and beyond, and he tells some of his stories later on in the book.

Times were still a-changing for the Regent building in the 1970s. Owners Rank turned the ballroom into a luxury cinema. A few years later Rank came up with another plan, this time to turn the theatre into a bingo hall. As those proposals didn't go down at all well with the Ipswich public, Rank had a re-think and the place remained East Anglia's premier live music venue. However, in 1988 the Regent was back in the headlines again when Rank announced plans to turn it into a five-screen cinema. The town's MP at the time, Jamie Cann, was horrified and launched a campaign to save the theatre as a live music venue. More than 30,000 people signed a petition and after months of talks Ipswich Borough Council struck a £4.2 million deal which saw the local authority buy the building.

1991 saw the gala re-opening of the Regent and it has remained in the council's hands ever since.

Left:
Theatre manager David Lowe breaks open the champagne after learning that his beloved Gaumont wasn't to be tuned into a bingo hall after all.

Below:
Stephen Foster (left) and David Kindred outside the Regent in 2004.

It still attracts some of the biggest names in the business. Suffolk's very own The Darkness opened the bill for Def Leppard before conquering the rock world. And in 2004, the year of its 75th anniversary, Pop Idol winner Will Young, singer and guitarist Chris Rea and young jazz sensation Jamie Cullum were just three of the big names to pack the place out.

The Regent has come a long way since opening with the all-talking film 'The Last Of Mrs. Cheyney'. Back in 1929 a seat to watch that in the front circle would have set you back 2s. 4d. These days fans of The Beach Boys have been quite happy to fork out £50 to see founder member Brian Wilson perform there.

For many it's the rock'n'roll years that hold the fondest memories so we hope you enjoy wallowing in nostalgia as we take you from Buddy to The Beatles…

Rave On

Remembering Buddy Holly and The Crickets

Buddy Holly and The Crickets were at the forefront of the American rock'n'roll movement and when they announced details of their first UK visit fans on this side of the pond couldn't wait to get their hands on tickets. Buddy and The Crickets had already hit the top of the UK charts with 'That'll Be The Day' while 'Oh Boy' and 'Peggy Sue' had both reached the Top 10. And with two more records - 'Listen To Me' and 'Maybe Baby' - entering the charts the day before Buddy's shows at the Gaumont his growing army of fans had plenty to look forward to.

In March 1958, Buddy, together with drummer Jerry Allison and bassist Joe B. Maudlin, rocked the joint to the delight of their mainly young audience. Ipswich had never witnessed music with such energy and Buddy's triumphant appearance in town whetted the appetite for more rock'n'roll shows at the Gaumont later that year.

By the end of 1958 Buddy Holly and The Crickets had gone their separate ways following Buddy's split with manager and producer Norman Petty. At the beginning of 1959 Buddy agreed to head a package tour with a back-up band which included Waylon Jennings who'd go on to become a big country music star. During that American tour tragedy struck when a plane taking Buddy, the Big Bopper and Richie Valens to their next gig crashed in a field near Mason City, Iowa killing all three. That was on 3rd February, which has become known as 'the day the music died'.

In actual fact Buddy Holly's music lives on and many fans of The Crickets turned out to see Jerry Allison and Joe B. Maudlin return to the Gaumont stage backing singer Nanci Griffith in May 1996. That was a truly memorable night made even better by the appearance of another Cricket - Sonny Curtis.

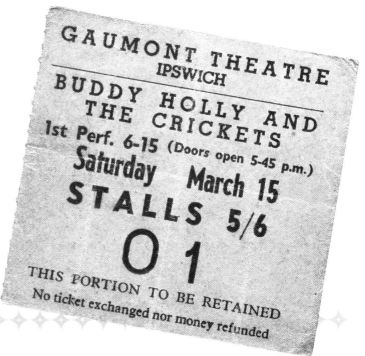

THE CRICKETS *Exclusive Coral Recording Artists*

COPYRIGHT

Above: *A rare signed publicity shot, signed backstage after the show at Ipswich. An identical publicity photo signed by Buddy and The Crickets at another venue on the same tour was sold for £908 at a London auction in July 2004.*

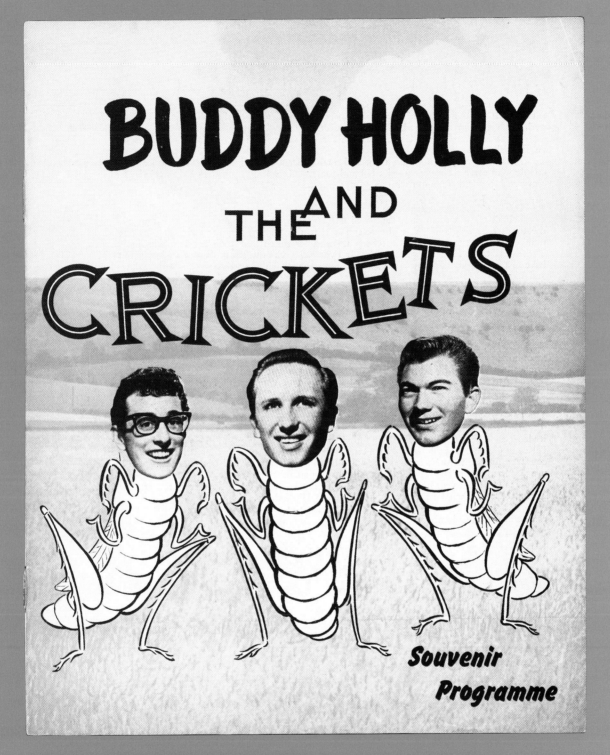

Buddy Holly souvenir programme for his first and only UK tour.

Personalities . . .

GARY MILLER

The story of Gary Miller, the singer who was an actor, is not one of a sudden "Gimmick" success. It is one of years of steady hard work and application to the job in hand. Less glamour, perhaps, but ultimately more lasting in its effect.

Special praise be to Gary, however, for one salient feature of his act—he sings songs with an English accent.

This quiet-spoken young man, still in his twenties, and his wife Joy, are a very sincere couple with three young sons—Pip, Kit and Jonty. Gary and Joy met in Italy while he was in the Navy and Joy had come out with an Army Entertainment Unit.

THE TANNER SISTERS

Fans often write to the Tanner Sisters, to ask why they cannot buy sheet music of any of the tunes they sing on TV. The reason is that the popular singing pair do not publish the numbers they write. They like to keep them exclusive, so that their act keeps its individuality.

Stella and Frances, who are in their twenties, have now written about twenty songs They have featured many of them on TV., a medium for which they give weeks of thought, planning and hard work to every number they sing. For they do not underestimate that a good T.V. appearance can make all the difference in the world to an artiste—as can a bad performance bring disaster. They do not design their act for the studio audience, but for the millions of viewers, working every camera move and angle to the lyrics.

RONNIE KEENE

Relaesed from the Army in 1947 when he joined Ken Mackintosh and his Band as a saxophone player, has played with Eric Winstone and his Orchestra and also Jack Parnell and his Orchestra. Formed his own band in 1956. Has broadcast regularly, appeared on B.B.C. T.V. 6.5 Special programme, and was also featured in the Frank Vaughan film "These Dangerous Years."

DES O'CONNOR

New young television star, who won first prize in a talent competition whilst he was serving with the R A.F., entered the theatrical profession after his demob when he became a Redcoat at Butlins Camps. He was spotted by a variety producer and made his debut at Newcastle Palace in October 1953. He has been eminently successful touring variety theatres throughout the country; first came to National notice when he appeared for six weeks in the commercial television programme "Spot The Tune" during the latter part of 1956.

During last year he was with the Lonnie Donegan show, and received rave notices in the National Press when he appeared at the London Hippodrome.

Versatile Des, a fine young comedian, is also the possessor of a very pleasant voice, which can be heard on Columbia records.

Pages from the souvenir programme for the Ipswich show.

RONNIE KEENE

TANNER SISTERS

BUDDY HOLLY

DES O'CONNOR

GARRY MILLER

PART ONE.

1. *Britain's new Musical sensation*

RONNIE KEENE and his Orchestra

PERSONNEL :

RONNIE KEENE, Leader/Tenor Saxophone ; HARRY SMITH, GORDON TURNBULL,
DAVE LOBAN, Trumpets ; JOHNNY WATSON, STEWART PARKER, Trombones ;
FRANK GILLESPIE, 1st Alto Saxophone ;   KEN LACK, 1st Tenor Saxophone ;
BILL BOYLE, 2nd Tenor Saxophone ; GEOFF ROBINSON, Baritone/Alto Saxophone ;
BILL WAYNE, Drummer ;   CLIVE CHAPLIN, Piano ;   RAY DUDDINGTON, Bass ;
LYNNE ADAMS, Vocalist.

ITEMS SELECTED FROM :

Woodchoppers Ball	**Sixty-Minute Man**
In the mood	**Gypsy in my soul**—Vocal, LYNNE ADAMS
	Blow that Saxophone

2. ## DES O'CONNOR introduces

3. ## THE TANNER SISTERS

ITEMS SELECTED FROM :

A Handful of Song	My Special Angel
Puttin' on the Style	At the Hop
Ma ! He's Making Eyes at Me	
Medley of Skiffle	Great Day
You are My Sunshine	I know that You know

4. *The Comedian with the modern style :*

DES O'CONNOR

5. *The Pye Nixa Recording Star*

GARY MILLER

ITEMS SELECTED FROM :

Wonderful, Wonderful	Story of My Life
A Light in the Window	Garden of Eden
	Green Door

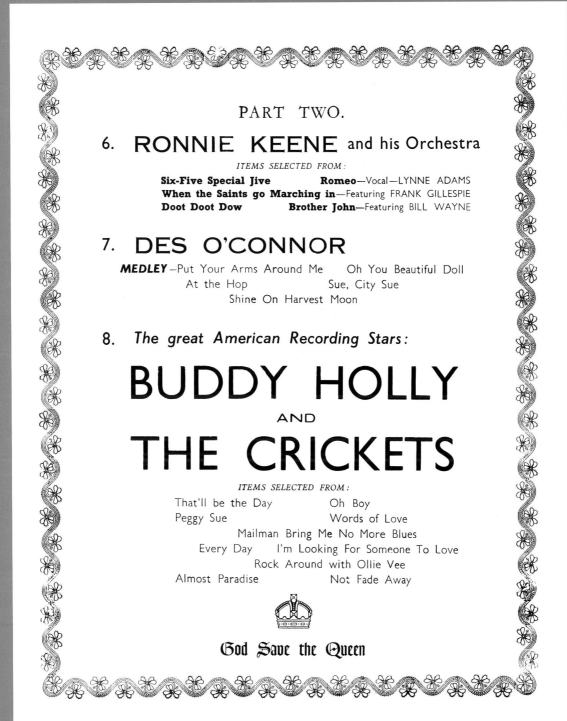

PART TWO.

6. RONNIE KEENE and his Orchestra

ITEMS SELECTED FROM:

Six-Five Special Jive   **Romeo**—Vocal—LYNNE ADAMS
When the Saints go Marching in—Featuring FRANK GILLESPIE
Doot Doot Dow   **Brother John**—Featuring BILL WAYNE

7. DES O'CONNOR

MEDLEY—Put Your Arms Around Me   Oh You Beautiful Doll
At the Hop   Sue, City Sue
Shine On Harvest Moon

8. *The great American Recording Stars:*

BUDDY HOLLY
AND
THE CRICKETS

ITEMS SELECTED FROM:

That'll be the Day   Oh Boy
Peggy Sue   Words of Love
Mailman Bring Me No More Blues
Every Day   I'm Looking For Someone To Love
Rock Around with Ollie Vee
Almost Paradise   Not Fade Away

God Save the Queen

BUDDY HOLLY and THE CRICKETS

The high-flying Buddy Holly and the Crickets, whose sensational best-selling recording of "That'll be the Day," written by themselves and recorded on the Coral label, catapulted this talented trio into the national spotlight.

As a result of their hit recording plus subsequent best sellers including "Oh, Boy," "Not Fade Away," "I'm Looking for Someone to Love," plus single hits by Buddy Holly including "Peggy Sue," "Everyday," etc., this sparkling trio, composed of Buddy Holly on guitar Joe Mauldin on bass and Jerry Allison on drums, have been in constant demand for personal and television appearances. Besides appearing in many of the leading showplaces throughout the country, they have appeared on many of the top American television shows, including the Ed Sullivan Show, twice, and the Arthur Murray Dance Party.

Buddy Holly was born on 7th September 1936, in Lubbock, Texas, and his musical career started at the ripe old age of eight when he started taking violin lessons. However, several squeaks later, Buddy decided his interest should be changed to the guitar. At the age of 15 the change was made and Buddy began singing while accompanying himself on guitar at various clubs throughout the southwest. He then headed for Nashville, Tenn., where he was signed by Decca Records and recorded western tunes.

After this, he visited the Norman Petty Recording Studios in Clovis, New Mexico, where with the help of Petty, who, incidentally, had a hit record of his own in "Almost Paradise," Buddy recorded a few of his own compositions. Petty took the demonstration records to Murray Deutsch of the Southern Music Publishing Company in New York, who in turn brought them to Bob Thiele of Coral and Bruns-wick Records, Thiele, immediately impressed, signed Buddy Holly and the Crickets to a recording contract with the Coral label, a subsidiary of Decca Records.

On the personal side, Buddy is five feet eleven inches tall, of slender build and weighs 145 pounds. He has curly black hair and the fire of youth in his attitude and performances.

Joe Mauldin, who plays bass, is the second member of the Crickets. Joe was born on 8th July 1939, and is a native of Lubbock, Texas. He is the smallest member of the group and stands five feet seven inches and weighs 140 pounds. Joe has blonde hair and hazel eyes and the handsome youngster's ambition is to someday own stocks and bonds in such companies as U.S. Steel and Standard Oil. His ambition should be soon realized judging by the quick success of the Crickets.

Rounding out the trio is Jerry Allison, the drummer, who hails from Hillsboro, Texas, where he was born on 31st August 1938. He moved from this small farming town to various sections of Texas, finally settling in Lubbock in 1950. Jerry has played drums at various clubs during his school days at Texas Tech in Lubbock, and when he was offered a job as a full-time musician touring the southern states, he promptly accepted. It wasn't long after that he met Buddy Holly, and the boys formed the nucleous of the trio. Jerry stands about six feet tall with wide shoulders, weighs 150 pounds, and has reddish-brown hair and blue eyes.

Hastings Printing Co., Portland Place, Hastings.   'Phone : Hastings 2450

Walk Right Back

✦✦

The Everly Brothers, Lonnie Donegan, Gene Vincent, Eddie Cochran and many more

American duo The Everly Brothers enjoyed enormous success on both sides of the Atlantic in the late fifties and the hits continued well into the mid sixties. Their appearance in Ipswich in 1960 came only days before the release of 'Cathy's Clown', the first single on the Warner Brothers label. A few weeks later the record reached number one in the charts.

Many other chart acts of that era performed in Ipswich and in this chapter, as well as recalling Phil and Don Everly's visit to Suffolk, we also look at some of the other big names to grace the Gaumont stage at around the time The Everlys were at their commercial peak.

GAUMONT THEATRE
IPSWICH

THE EVERLY BROTHERS
1st Performance 6-15
MONDAY **4**
APRIL
STALLS 5/6

ZI 44

No ticket exchanged nor money refunded
THIS PORTION TO BE RETAINED

The undisputed king of skiffle was a Glaswegian-born musician who took part of his stage name from American bluesman Lonnie Johnson. That was back in 1952 when Tony Donegan was on the same bill as Johnson and the confused compere introduced him as Lonnie Donegan. Donegan rather liked his new stage name and adopted it from that night onwards.

Skiffle took the nation by storm in 1956 and although the style of music itself was rather short-lived Lonnie Donegan's popularity showed

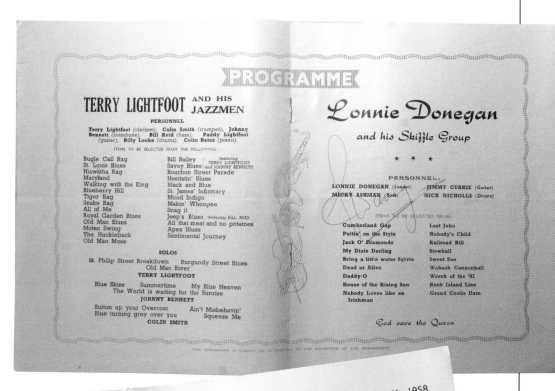

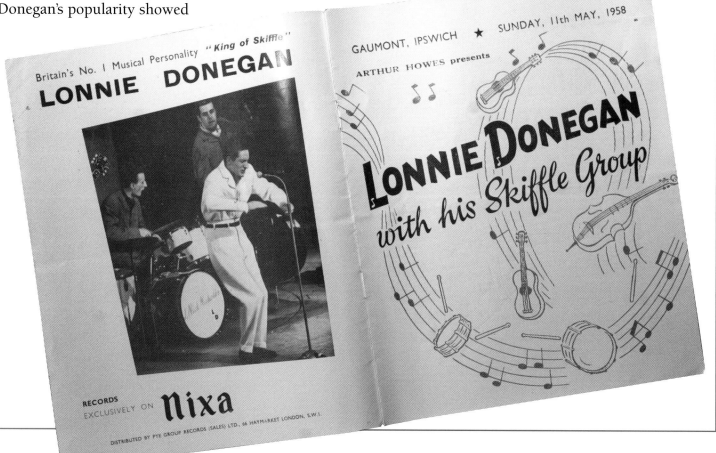

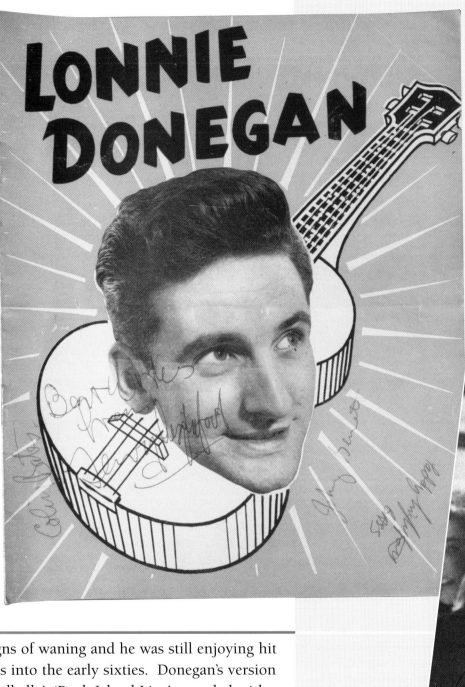

Despite numerous health problems Lonnie Donegan's career lasted into the new Millennium. In fact, right up until his death in February 2002 he was again filling the sort of venues he'd originally packed out in his heyday. A sell-out show at the Regent in Ipswich was to be one of his last. Later on during that tour he died following a show in Peterborough.

LONNIE DONEGAN CLUB
34, GREEK STREET, LONDON, W.I.

no signs of waning and he was still enjoying hit singles into the early sixties. Donegan's version of Leadbelly's 'Rock Island Line' recorded with jazz star Chris Barber marked the start of the skiffle era and introduced many thousands of people to American folk and blues. Skiffle bands were formed in every town and city in the UK, the most successful being The Vipers and Chas McDevitt's Skiffle Group.

Joe Brown on stage at the Gaumont with young fans.

Joe Brown

Laughing Joe Brown is a typical, happy-go-lucky product of London's Cockney East End. He has that rare quality of super personality which caused him to leap to fame overnight on Television. Aged just 18 he joined the Marty Wilde T.V. show *Boy Meets Girls* as a guitarist but his tremendous verve for life could not be contained and he shot in a matter of weeks from musician to a leading personality and comic on the show. The success story of Joe Brown is a true life "rags to riches" tale—for at 13 he was a spare-time rag and bone merchant. On leaving school at fifteen Joe devoted most of his time to his beloved guitar. In time his reputation as a guitarist spread, in the autumn of 1959 word of his ability reached rock 'n' roll impresario Larry Parnes, who booked him in a spot in a show at Southend. That was the beginning of the meteoric rise to fame of Joe Brown.

— 4 —

Joe Brown was one of those many youngsters who'd started out in skiffle groups but he had to wait until 1962 before becoming a household name. He and his band The Bruvvers played the Gaumont in October 1963 having enjoyed a massive hit the previous year with 'A Picture Of You'. He was back at the venue five months later by which time he'd added to his tally of hits. Today he remains a respected performer so much so that he was invited to appear at the George Harrison memorial concert at The Royal Albert Hall in London.

JOE BROWN

In 1960 rock'n'roll legends Gene Vincent and Eddie Cochran came to town. It was part of a UK visit that was to end in tragedy when 21 year old Cochran was killed in a car crash at Chippenham in Wiltshire on April 17th. He was on his way to the airport to return home after a hugely successful three months of stage and TV appearances.

Right:

Autographed programme pictures from the Ipswich show.

Vincent was in the same car but escaped with only bad bruising. The ironically-titled 'Three Steps To Heaven' was released soon after Cochran's death and topped the charts. His death was a huge loss and his influence is still heard in the music of today.

EDDIE COCHRAN

This is his first ever trip to England

Gene Vincent was back in Ipswich sooner than his fans might have been expecting. After going home to the States to get over the loss of Cochran - one of his closest friends - Vincent decided to return to Britain to build on the success he'd already enjoyed. Joining him on the tour were Freddy Cannon and Jerry Keller. Cannon's 'Way Down Yonder In New Orleans' had earlier that year reached number three in the UK charts while Keller's number one from 1959, 'Here Comes Summer', meant he too was well known to British record buyers.

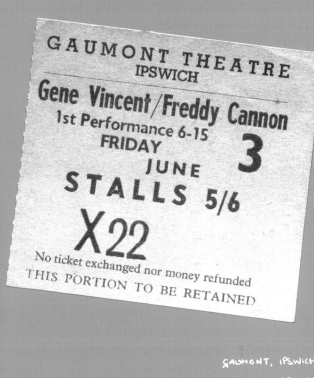

GAUMONT THEATRE
IPSWICH
Gene Vincent / Freddy Cannon
1st Performance 6-15
FRIDAY
JUNE 3
STALLS 5/6
X22
No ticket exchanged nor money refunded
THIS PORTION TO BE RETAINED

GAUMONT, IPSWICH 3-6-60.
JERRY KELLER

JERRY LEE LEWIS

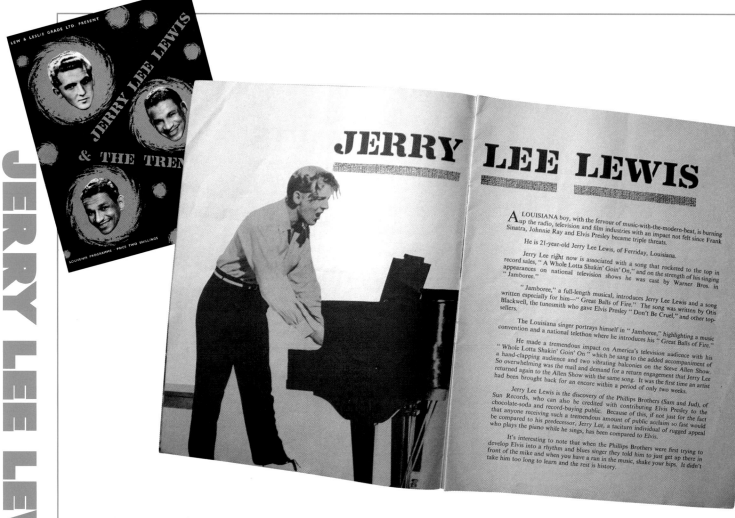

LEW & LESLIE GRADE LTD. PRESENT

JERRY LEE LEWIS & THE TRENIERS

SOUVENIR PROGRAMME · PRICE TWO SHILLINGS

JERRY LEE LEWIS

A LOUISIANA boy, with the fervour of music-with-the-modern-beat, is burning up the radio, television and film industries with an impact not felt since Frank Sinatra, Johnnie Ray and Elvis Presley became triple threats.

He is 21-year-old Jerry Lee Lewis, of Ferriday, Louisiana.

Jerry Lee right now is associated with a song that rocketed to the top in record sales, " A Whole Lotta Shakin' Goin' On," and on the strength of his singing appearances on national television shows he was cast by Warner Bros. in " Jamboree."

" Jamboree," a full-length musical, introduces Jerry Lee Lewis and a song written especially for him—" Great Balls of Fire." The song was written by Otis Blackwell, the tunesmith who gave Elvis Presley " Don't Be Cruel," and other top-sellers.

The Louisiana singer portrays himself in " Jamboree," highlighting a music convention and a national telethon where he introduces his " Great Balls of Fire."

He made a tremendous impact on America's television audience with his " Whole Lotta Shakin' Goin' On " which he sang to the added accompaniment of a hand-clapping audience and two vibrating balconies on the Steve Allen Show. So overwhelming was the mail and demand for a return engagement that Jerry Lee returned again to the Allen Show with the same song. It was the first time an artist had been brought back for an encore within a period of only two weeks.

Jerry Lee Lewis is the discovery of the Phillips Brothers (Sam and Jud), of Sun Records, who can also be credited with contributing Elvis Presley to the chocolate-soda and record-buying public. Because of this, if not just for the fact that anyone receiving such a tremendous amount of public acclaim so fast would be compared to his predecessor, Jerry Lee, a taciturn individual of rugged appeal who plays the piano while he sings, has been compared to Elvis.

It's interesting to note that when the Phillips Brothers were first trying to develop Elvis into a rhythm and blues singer they told him to just get up there in front of the mike and when you have a run in the music, shake your hips. It didn't take him too long to learn and the rest is history.

Back in 1958 the man known as 'The Killer' unleashed his no-holds-barred live show on the British public but his planned 37-date tour didn't last long. It soon emerged that a few months earlier Jerry Lee Lewis had secretly wed his 13 year old cousin Myra Gale Brown. To make matters worse he was still married to another woman and when the story broke in the UK very early into the tour Lewis found himself at the centre of a big scandal and was forced to return home. Sadly for his fans in Ipswich his proposed appearance at the Gaumont was one of many that were pulled. His American co-headliners, The Treniers, carried on with the tour and on all accounts put on a memorable show but drafting in Chas McDevitt and Terry Wayne was scant consolation for those fans hoping to see the man who in 1957 had taken 'Great Balls Of Fire' to the top of the charts.

GAUMONT THEATRE
IPSWICH

JERRY LEE LEWIS
and the TRENIERS

1st Performance at 6—20
Friday   June 13

STALLS 4/6

Z1 19

THIS PORTION TO BE RETAINED
No ticket exchanged nor money refunded

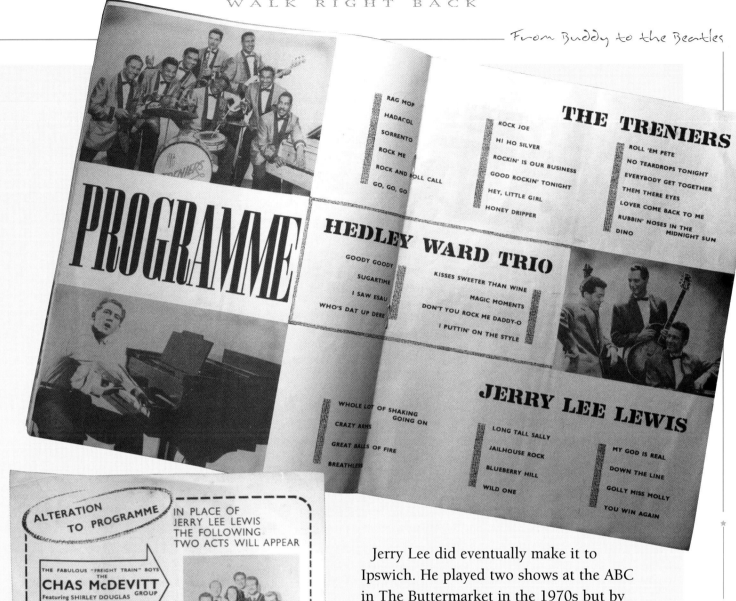

THE TRENIERS

ROCK JOE
HI HO SILVER
ROCKIN' IS OUR BUSINESS
GOOD ROCKIN' TONIGHT
HEY, LITTLE GIRL
HONEY DRIPPER

ROLL 'EM PETE
NO TEARDROPS TONIGHT
EVERYBODY GET TOGETHER
THEM THERE EYES
LOVER COME BACK TO ME
RUBBIN' NOSES IN THE MIDNIGHT SUN
DINO

RAG MOP
HADACOL
SORRENTO
ROCK ME
ROCK AND ROLL CALL
GO, GO, GO

HEDLEY WARD TRIO

GOODY GOODY
SUGARTIME
I SAW ESAU
WHO'S DAT UP DERE

KISSES SWEETER THAN WINE
MAGIC MOMENTS
DON'T YOU ROCK ME DADDY-O
I PUTTIN' ON THE STYLE

JERRY LEE LEWIS

WHOLE LOT OF SHAKING GOING ON
CRAZY ARMS
GREAT BALLS OF FIRE
BREATHLESS

LONG TALL SALLY
JAILHOUSE ROCK
BLUEBERRY HILL
WILD ONE

MY GOD IS REAL
DOWN THE LINE
GOLLY MISS MOLLY
YOU WIN AGAIN

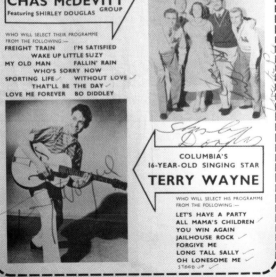

ALTERATION TO PROGRAMME — IN PLACE OF JERRY LEE LEWIS THE FOLLOWING TWO ACTS WILL APPEAR

THE FABULOUS "FREIGHT TRAIN" BOYS
THE CHAS McDEVITT GROUP
Featuring SHIRLEY DOUGLAS

WHO WILL SELECT THEIR PROGRAMME FROM THE FOLLOWING —
FREIGHT TRAIN   I'M SATISFIED
WAKE UP LITTLE SUZY
MY OLD MAN   FALLIN' RAIN
WHO'S SORRY NOW
SPORTING LIFE   WITHOUT LOVE
THAT'LL BE THE DAY
LOVE ME FOREVER   BO DIDDLEY

COLUMBIA'S 16-YEAR-OLD SINGING STAR
TERRY WAYNE

WHO WILL SELECT HIS PROGRAMME FROM THE FOLLOWING —
LET'S HAVE A PARTY
ALL MAMA'S CHILDREN
YOU WIN AGAIN
JAILHOUSE ROCK
FORGIVE ME
LONG TALL SALLY
OH LONESOME ME
STOOD UP

Jerry Lee did eventually make it to Ipswich. He played two shows at the ABC in The Buttermarket in the 1970s but by then he'd all but turned his back on rock'n'roll. He insisted on playing mainly country and western songs and was promptly booed by some members of the audience. He did do a medley of his classic Sun rock'n'roll hits but this simply highlighted his apparent disregard for the songs that had made him famous.

Johnny Duncan

Johnny Duncan and his band The Blue Grass Boys were best known in the UK for their 1957 hit 'Last Train to San Fernando'. His show at the Gaumont followed what turned out to be his final hit 'Footprints In the Snow'. He was joined on the tour by Terry Lightfoot's Jazzmen and The King Brothers.

GAUMONT THEATRE
IPSWICH
JOHNNY DUNCAN
1st Perf. 5-30 (Doors open 5-0 p.m.)
Sunday January 26
STALLS 3/-
Z2 35
THIS PORTION TO BE RETAINED
No ticket exchanged nor money refunded

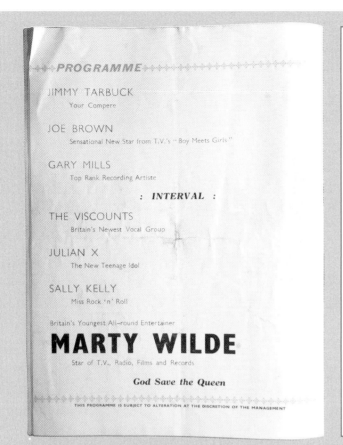

MARTY WILDE

Working in a South London timber yard did'nt give Marty Wilde much prospect of buying the sports car he longed for. He saw it gleaming in a showroom near his blackened house in Woolwich Road, Greenwich, but at thirty shillings a week he reckoned on it taking him seven years before he could buy it. So Marty, six foot three 19 years of age, drew out his savings, walked into a second-hand music shop and speculated in an old guitar.

He learned to play it in three months and hot-footed it into Soho to sing for his supper in the glittering land of Espresso coffee bars and chip shops. Marty got a Pound a night for his troubles; then along came Larry Parnes, co-handler of Britain's rock-'n'-roll king, Tommy Steele. Larry signed up Marty, plucked him off the coffee counters and placed him for a season at a chic West End night club.

First nighters included Josephine Douglas, boss of the successful B.B.C. T.V. teenage show "Six-Five Special." Marty impressed her with his version of "Honeycomb." He got a spot on the show and drew 167 fan letters.

Mr. Johnny Franz, Recording Manager for Philips Records, saw the show, invited Marty to a recording test and signed him within 30 minutes of hearing the tapes.

His first record, "Honeycomb," backed by his own composition "Wildcat," is already a hit.

Then Marty stunned show-business by announcing he could not take on many Sunday concerts because of his commitments at a local church. He played each Sunday to young children while the organ was being repaired.

But the rock-'n'-roll Sunday School teacher shared top billing at the huge Trocadero Cinema, Elephant and Castle, with the Deep River Boys a few Sundays later.

Now Marty has swapped his bundle of plywood for a £200 guitar.

Marty has bright blue eyes, likes Italian food — and sports cars.

His father is a London bus driver.

The final sensation in his success spiral came five minutes before his second T.V. appearance. A film producer rang him with an offer to appear in a leading role.

Impresario Larry Parnes was a key figure on the British pop scene in the late fifties/early sixties and thanks to programmes like 'Oh Boy' and '6-5 Special' his stable of young male singers got plenty of TV exposure. Londoner Marty Wilde notched up a string of hits and became a regular visitor to the Gaumont as part of package tours which also featured the likes of Georgie Fame, Joe Brown and Billy Fury.

Rock'n Trad Spectacular

THE NEW
NOISE OF
1960

STARRING
Billy Fury AND HIS
COMPANY OF 50

SOUVENIR PROGRAMME   ONE SHILLING

VINCE EAGER

Handsome Vince Eager is the dandy of rock 'n' roll singers. He likes expensive clothes, food and fun. His large wardrobe is crammed with suits, shirts and a vast array of ties. The lights of West End London have a compelling fascination for him. But at 19 Vince Eager is a polished man of the world, a show business personality and a singer with a stage and television reputation that many an older artiste might envy.

It is but a short time ago that Vince emerged from the Sherwood Forest country, an inexperienced, untried country lad.

Larry Parnes spotted him competing in the finals of a nation-wide talent contest. Twenty-four hours later he was under contract. Success was instant. Vince was a rave in Paris and in London. Television clamoured for his services. He has appeared regularly in "OH BOY" and "SIX FIVE SPECIAL" and was the resident star of "DRUMBEAT".

Six feet three inches tall, Vince Eager hails from Grantham. His height and good looks have made him enormously popular with teenage fans all over the country. Traffic is often brought to a standstill when crowds gather outside theatres where he is appearing. Vince Eager is a young man who is going places.

Left:

*Georgie Fame
and his autograph.*

GAUMONT THEATRE
IPSWICH
MARTY WILDE
1st Performance 5-30
SUNDAY
NOVEMBER 8
CIRCLE 5/-
J 2
No ticket exchanged nor money refunded
THIS PORTION TO BE RETAINED

The Everly Brothers were without doubt the finest pop duo of their time and very few, if any, acts have come close to reaching the standards their harmonies set.

Kentucky-based Don and Phil were the sons of radio performers Ike and Margaret Everly and appeared on family shows until their parents retired. In 1955 the brothers went to Nashville in search of fame and fortune. It took them many months to establish themselves in Music City but their patience eventually paid off when they were signed as songwriters by Roy Acuff and Wesley Rose. Acuff and Rose secured them a recording deal with Cadence Records and in 1957, having recorded 'Bye Bye Love', they made their debut on Nashville's Grand Ole Opry. Within weeks The Everlys had sold a million copies of 'Bye Bye Love' and for the next five years were rarely out of the pop and country charts.

THE EVERLYS' UK TOP 10 HITS

Bye Bye Love
Wake Up Little Susie
All I Have To Dream/Claudette
Bird Dog
Problems
('Til) I Kissed You
Cathy's Clown
When Will I Be Loved
Lucille/ So Sad (To Watch
   Good Love Go Bad)
Walk Right Back/Ebony Eyes
Temptation
Crying In the Rain
The Price of Love

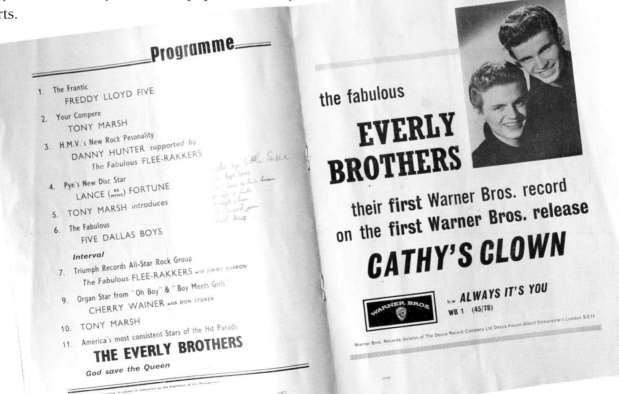

They were voted the top group in the world by readers of *The New Musical Express* in 1958 and were the first duo to be inducted into the Rock and Roll Hall of Fame.

The Everly Brothers' sound proved inspirational to Paul Simon and Art Garfunkel. When Don and Phil were breaking through, Simon and Garfunkel were plying their trade in New York as Tom and Jerry! It was obvious that Paul and Art had modelled their vocal style on their heroes and ironically just as The Everly Brothers' hits were drying up Simon and Garfunkel took over as America's favourite singing duo. In the summer of 2004 Simon and Garfunkel played a handful of outdoor shows in the UK and invited The Everly Brothers to join them as their special guests. It was a match made in heaven.

Left: *The Everlys with singer Tommy Bruce (centre)*

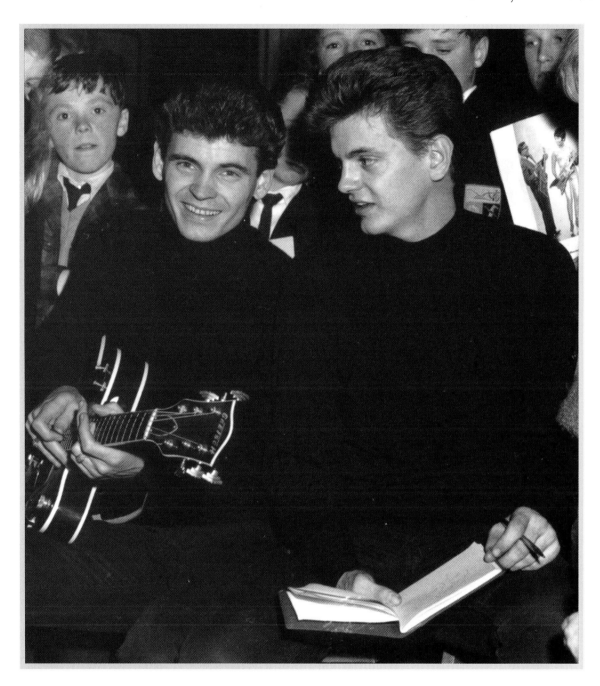

The Everly Brothers

Lifelong Everly Brothers fan Stan Singleton clutching his 1960 tour programme and the duo's autographs.

As a teenager Stan attended virtually all of the rock'n'roll shows at the Gaumont and thankfully he still has most of the memorabilia.

During the rock'n'roll era Ipswich-born Stan frequently travelled to London to catch those stars of the day who didn't include Suffolk on their tour itinerary. He was often joined by school chum Bryan Knights who went on to become a head teacher

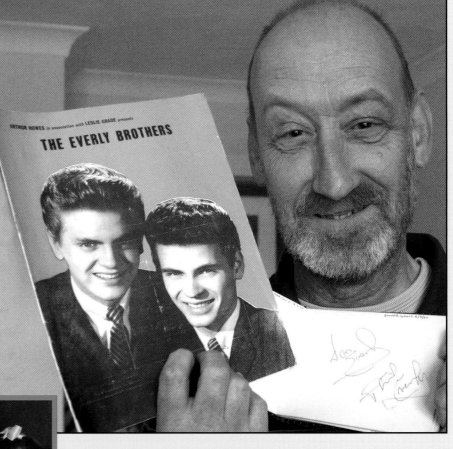

before combining that role with football commentaries for SGR FM and most recently BBC Radio Suffolk.

Stan remains an avid music fan and was first in the queue for tickets when Beach Boy Brian Wilson announced he was coming to the Regent in the summer of 2004.

Left:

New Orleans rock'n'roll legend Little Richard takes time out backstage at the Gaumont to sign autographs for some of his youngest fans. He is pictured in front of the stage door which leads out into Woodbridge Road.

Phil and Don did make a return to the Gaumont in 1963 when they topped a bill that also included Bo Diddley, Little Richard, The Rolling Stones and Mickie Most.

Long after the hits dried up The Everly Brothers proved their pulling power yet again by selling the theatre out in the 1980s. Backed by a band featuring top British session men like guitarist Albert Lee and keyboards player Pete Wingfield, they'd lost none of their distinctive harmonic sound.

When Mickie Most's singing career failed to take off he became a hugely successful record producer enjoying immediate success with The Animals before steering the careers of other sixties stars like Herman's Hermits, Lulu, Jeff Beck and Donovan. He certainly had the Midas touch. He formed his own record label, RAK , and many of his hit-makers in the 1970s appeared at the Gaumont. Acts like Hot Chocolate, Mud and Suzi Quatro packed the place out. Mickie became one of Britain's wealthiest businessmen. He died in August 2003, just three weeks short of his 65th birthday.

The Victor Sylvester Dance Studio was one of the most popular places to go for the teenagers of the late 1950s and early 1960s. It was run by instructors Bob Morley and Rita Carlton who taught hundreds of people how to waltz, tango, jive and twist. Our selection of photos captures the era perfectly.

Left and below:
Regulars at the Regent twisting the night away.

Below:
*Let's have a party -
fun and games at 'Vic's'.*

38

I'm Into Something Good

David Lowe:
the man who made it all happen

David Lowe's love affair with the Gaumont Theatre began in 1958 and although he retired as manager there in 1989 the theatre still holds a huge place in his heart.

David started his career in show business at the Regal cinema in North Walsham in Norfolk where he was a projectionist. His brother was also in the business at The Astoria in Finsbury Park and David begged him

to let him go and work there with him. Shortly after that his brother left to go into the airforce which left David, who was still only 16, on his own in north London. David enjoyed his job there and after learning a great deal about the business was drafted into the army in 1943. Four years later he was back in the

Right: *Peter Noone and the rest of Herman's Hermits joining David in celebrating Ipswich Town's promotion back to the top flight. Bill McGarry's team had just clinched the Second Division title. This picture shows Peter and David holding a copy of The Football Star, known as The Green 'Un. The visit of Herman's Hermits came in May 1968 and they had plenty to celebrate in the way of chart success too. Their current single 'Sleepy Joe' was in the Top 20. Four years earlier they'd enjoyed a number one with 'I'm Into Something Good' and at one point in the sixties they were as successful as The Beatles in the United States. Also in the picture (front right) is support act Dave Berry who enjoyed three Top Five hits in the mid-sixties.*

business training to be a cinema manager. His first port of call was the Odeon in Ipswich and after spending three months there he had stints in Norwich, Bury St. Edmunds and Colchester. He was eventually appointed manager of the Hippodrome in Colchester and it was during his time there that he was offered the job at the Gaumont. David said:

> I'd been there for three years when one day my boss came in and said he wanted to talk to me about something very serious. I thought what does he mean, something serious? He asked me if we would like to go to the Gaumont, Ipswich. I knew the place having done a few odd days as relief manager, so I said yes and arrived at the place in March 1958. I thought this place has a future because not only did it have films, it also had shows and it was the start of what we call the big shows.

Top left: *Gerry Marsden of Gerry and the Pacemakers fame giving the Lowe family a quick guitar lesson on the Gaumont stage. The group was in town at the start of 1964 appearing in the pantomime 'Babes In The Wood'. They had just become the first act to reach number one with their first three records - 'How Do You Do It?', 'I Like It' and 'You'll Never Walk Alone'. It was a record that stood until 1984 when fellow Liverpudlians Frankie Goes To Hollywood equalled their feat.*

Bottom left: *Crooner Frankie Vaughan during one of his many appearances in Ipswich. A variety show veteran, Frankie was awarded an OBE for his charity work.*

Left: *Renewing his friendship with Cliff Richard. This was the third time they'd been photographed together.*

Cliff was knighted in 1995 and is the only artist to have enjoyed British number ones in five different decades.

Left: *Another award coming David's way. A top manager accolade from Rank presented by The Searchers who notched up a few achievements of their own including two number ones in 1964 - 'Needles And Pins' and 'Don't Throw Your Love Away'. They were tipped to be as big as The Beatles. Also pictured (second from left) is the singer Big Dee Irwin, best known for his 1963 hit 'Swinging On A Star'.*

Right: *Seventies pop star David Essex raising a glass before one of his many sell-out shows at the Gaumont. He officially opened the foyer bar. It might be 30 years since he was a teen idol but the London-born singer remains a big favourite with the ladies.*

Below: *David introduces another seventies star - Leo Sayer - to a couple of fans backstage in 1977. Earlier that year Leo had hit the chart summit with the ballad 'When I Need You'.*

David Lowe had a memorable start as manager of the Gaumont Theatre. His first show was Buddy Holly's concert there on 15th March 1958 and it just got better and better. He became good friends with skiffle legend Lonnie Donegan taking him for a social visit to RAF Bentwaters before his shows at the Gaumont. Also at around this time he met rock'n'roll stars Gene Vincent, Eddie Cochran and the Everly Brothers as well as the young English singing stars of the day like Cliff Richard, Marty Wilde and Joe Brown. It must have been difficult to keep up with all the top names appearing at his theatre.

Above: *American singer Gene Pitney turning back the clock to a previous visit to one of his favourite theatres. Also pictured is the Mayor of Ipswich, Councillor Peter Gardiner and his wife Sue.*

Left: *Country music legend Tammy Wynette standing by her man! David watches on as Tammy admires a cake baked to mark the theatre's 50th anniversary. Tammy was one of many country superstars to grace the Gaumont in the seventies and eighties. Among the others were Glen Campbell, Billie Jo Spears and Don Williams.*

Tammy Wynette

Then just when it looked like things couldn't get any better along came The Beatles and The Rolling Stones and a whole host of other groups who had become household names. His only regret is not keeping all the posters and souvenir programmes:

At the time you don't know all these people are going to become legends. A Beatles poster from around the time they came to Ipswich went for three and a half grand recently. We threw a lot of those away at the time. You simply couldn't keep everything. We did give a lot away but we couldn't keep posters hanging around, they were a fire hazard.

David Lowe ran the Gaumont for more than thirty years and became known as 'Mr Gaumont'. He's rightly proud of the part he played in putting the venue on the live music map. He's also chuffed that local organisations such as The Ipswich Co-op Juniors, The Ipswich Operatic and Dramatic Society and The Ipswich Gilbert and Sullivan Society all graced the stage during his time there. The Ipswich Civic Concerts were particular favourites of his too.

All I Really Want to Do

The Byrds, The Shadows and Ipswich's own Nick and the Nomads

Some of the biggest pop groups of the sixties came to Ipswich and many of them graced the Gaumont stage. Later on in this book we cover visits by The Beatles, The Rolling Stones and The Kinks. In this chapter we recall visits by The Byrds and The Shadows and bring you the story of how Ipswich's very own Nick and the Nomads followed in the footsteps of The Beatles. We also remember the days of Dusty Springfield and some of the other singing stars who delighted the Ipswich concert-goers.

Left: *The Byrds backstage at The Gaumont in August 1965. Pictured left to right are drummer Michael Clarke, guitarists and singers David Crosby and Roger McGuinn, bassist and vocalist Chris Hillman and singer Gene Clark.*

Above: *Isle Of Wight-born Craig Douglas at the height of his success in the early sixties. His most successful single was 'Only Sixteen' which topped the charts in 1959, the year in which he was also voted Best New Singer.*

Right:
Craig Douglas's autograph.

Far right: *English rock'n'roll star Wee Willie Harris. Although he was a well known figure on the British music scene, he never enjoyed chart success. He'd often colour his hair purple or orange! He's been described as the link between music hall and rock'n'roll and was given a name-check by Ian Dury on his 1979 hit 'Reasons To be Cheerful (Part 3)'.*

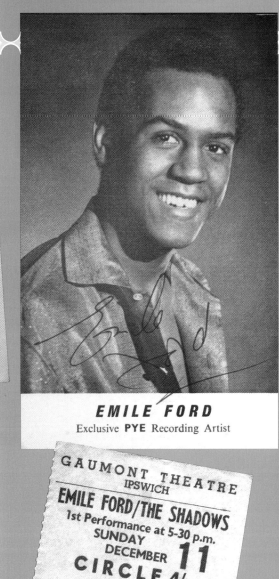

EMILE FORD
Exclusive **PYE** Recording Artist

GAUMONT THEATRE
IPSWICH
EMILE FORD/THE SHADOWS
1st Performance at 5-30 p.m.
SUNDAY
DECEMBER
11
CIRCLE 4/-
M12
No ticket exchanged nor money refunded
THIS PORTION TO BE RETAINED

The Shadows were Britain's most successful instrumental group, having originally backed Cliff Richard. Their visit in the run up to Christmas 1960 was one of many they made to the theatre throughout their long time together. In fact, they included a sell-out date at the Regent on their farewell tour in 2004. Forty-four years earlier they were co-headliners there with Emile Ford and the Checkmates who were in the charts at the time with 'Counting Teardrops'. The previous year Emile's 'What Do You Want To Make Those Eyes At Me For?' reached number one in the UK charts.

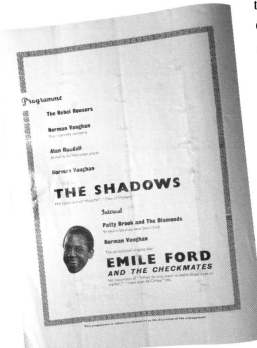

Left:
*The Shadows'
autographs
from Ipswich.*

47

Top left:

Billy J Kramer in demand backstage at the Gaumont in September 1964. At the time Billy and his group the Dakotas were enjoying their sixth top ten hit 'From A Window', yet another song written by John Lennon and Paul McCartney.

Top right:

Chart-topping teenager Helen Shapiro busy signing autographs prior to her show in Ipswich in November 1963. It was her first visit to town having the previous year made a dramatic breakthrough with 'Walking Back To Happiness' and 'You Don't Know'. Both singles made number one, making her the youngest female singer to have topped the UK charts. On her first UK tour The Beatles were one of her support acts!

Above:
Singer turned actor Adam Faith. He returned to the Gaumont in the 1970s but not as a performer. At that time he was managing Leo Sayer. Faith died in March 2003.

Left:

Gene Pitney's UK success story began in 1961 and by the time this photograph was taken in February 1969 he'd amassed no fewer than 16 British hits. And more were to come including a surprise number one with Marc Almond of Soft Cell in 1989.

Left:

Ladies man Engelbert Humperdinck pictured before his show in Ipswich in 1967. He was at the peak of his popularity having earlier in the year enjoyed two number ones - 'Release Me' and 'The Last Waltz'.

Over the next eight pages we feature programme covers and posters from the classic rock 'n' roll years at the Gaumont.

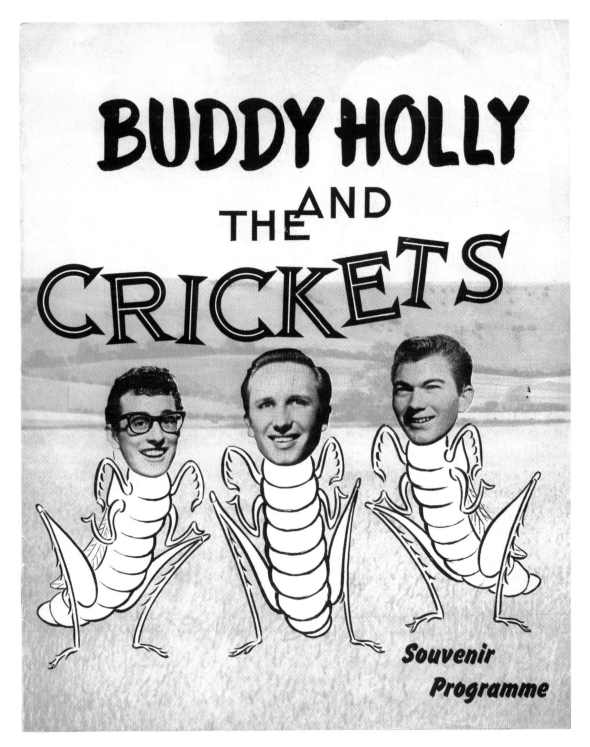

Buddy Holly and The Crickets from March 1958.

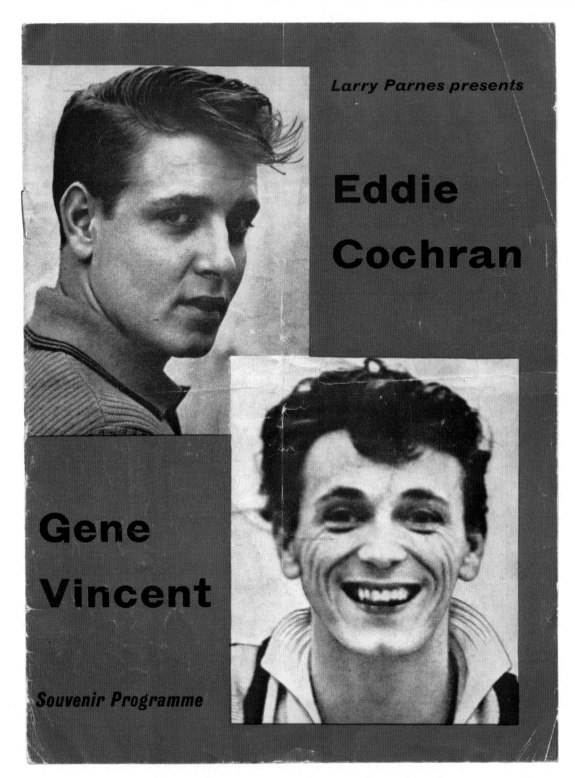

Eddie Cochran and Gene Vincent from January 1960.

Jerry Lee Lewis and The Treniers.
Because of the scandal surrounding his marriage Jerry Lee did not make his scheduled appearance at Ipswich in June 1958.

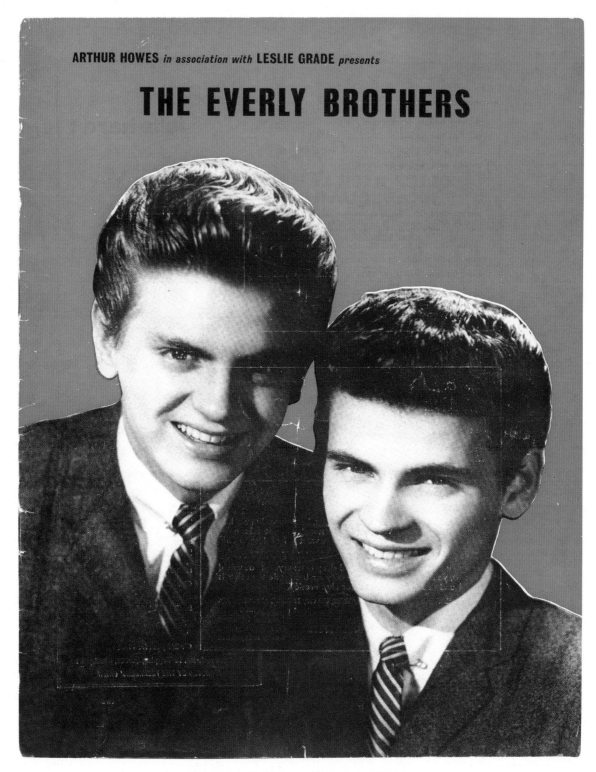

The Everly Brothers cover from April 1960.

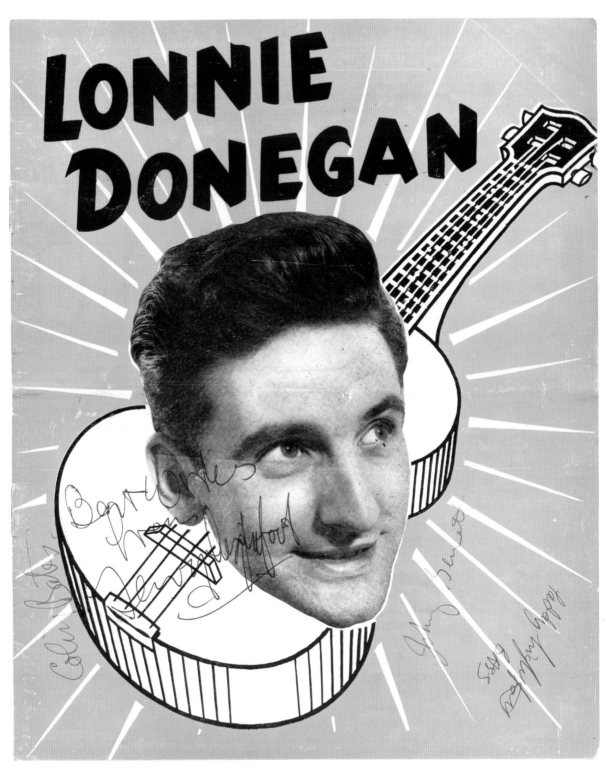

Lonnie Donegan, May 1958.

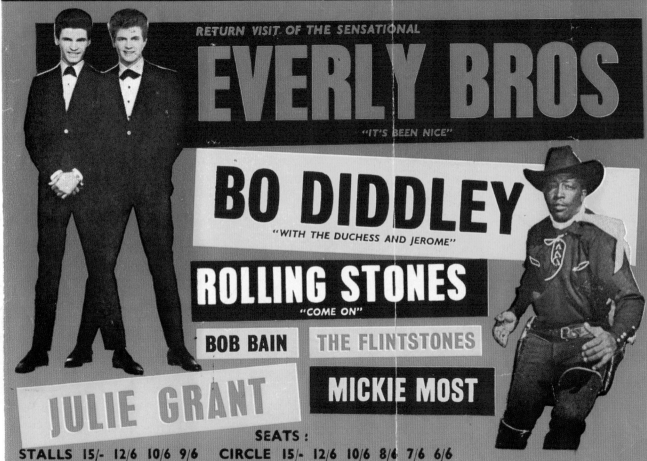

A poster for the Everly Brothers show of November 1963.

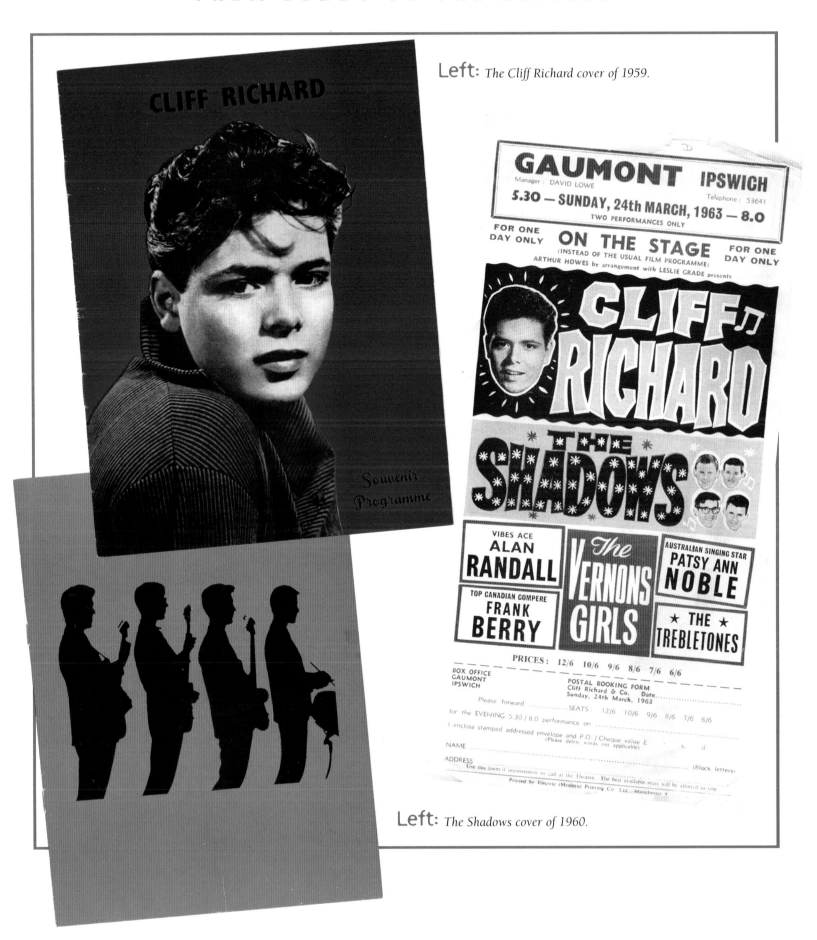

Left: *The Cliff Richard cover of 1959.*

Left: *The Shadows cover of 1960.*

The Beatles cover of October 1964.

Dusty Springfield was one of the biggest names of the sixties. Her soulful, husky voice was rarely out of the charts once she had established herself as a solo artist with the top 5 hit 'I Only Want To be With You'.

She made her first visit to Ipswich three years earlier as a member of singing group The Springfields (pictured right). They were in town as part of The Charlie Drake Show in February 1961.

She was next at the Gaumont in 1964 when she appeared as a star in her own right. In fact, Ipswich had a double dose of Dusty that year. She was in town in March and then returned in December.

Gaumont manager David Lowe recalls the time Dusty's manager sent him out to buy a china tea-set for the star of the show:

I thought I'd better get the best I could for Dusty but her manager insisted I get the cheapest I could find. So I went to Footman's in the town centre and got one for 19s 6d which was still quite a lot but by no means the most expensive. When I got it back to the dressing room Dusty's manager told me that would do nicely. 'Don't worry', he said, 'at the end of the show Dusty likes to throw the cups and saucers against the dressing room walls. It's her way of unwinding!'

Dusty's career took something of a nosedive in the 1970s but thanks to collaborations with The Pet Shop Boys in the late 1980s she enjoyed a new lease of chart life. She died in March 1999.

THE BYRDS

When American group The Byrds hit The Gaumont stage they were at the peak of their powers. They played Ipswich in August 1965 by which time their version of Bob Dylan's 'Mr. Tambourine Man' had taken the UK charts by storm. It had been at number one back in June and as they arrived in Ipswich the single 'All I Really Want To Do' was in the top ten.

Hugely influential, The Byrds would go on to record more memorable records like 'Turn! Turn! Turn!' and 'Eight Miles High' before eventually disbanding in 1973.

Fans in Ipswich were lucky enough to see what many regard as the classic Byrds line-up - Roger McGuinn (below left), David Crosby (above right), Gene Clark (facing page), Michael Clarke (below right) and Chris Hillman (below centre).

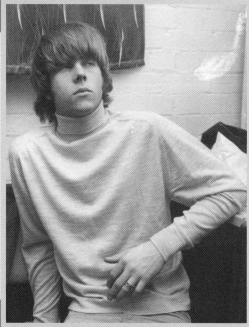

THE BYRDS

Below:
The Byrds with young fans in a tiny room under the Gaumont stage.

Ipswich's very own Nick and the Nomads came so close to stardom they could almost touch it. They formed in 1962 and quickly made their mark locally packing out various Ipswich venues. The band also followed in the footsteps of The Beatles playing to enthusiastic audiences in Hamburg, Germany. They won an audition for the trip during an all-day session for local bands held at The Gaumont. Recalling their month-long trip to Hamburg, band member Roy Clover said:

An ITV crew followed us around and we were featured on a programme called 'Roving Report'.

They did lots of scenes of us at The Top Ten Club. The whole programme was on us. We played the raw side of rock'n'roll. It was a great time.

When Nick and the Nomads returned to the UK they clinched a record deal with HMV Records releasing a single 'You're Nobody Till Somebody Loves You'. The band toured with groups like The Hollies and Manfred Mann. But it was not to be and later in 1964 they split. It had been a whirlwind two years together and forty years later music fans in and around Ipswich still talk fondly of them.

Left:

Hamburg here we come! Nick and the Nomads celebrate their trip to Germany after winning the audition at the Gaumont in the spring of 1964. This picture was taken on the same spot where the Beatles were interviewed later the same year. From left are Ron West, Ben Foster, Nick Wymer, Dave Cutting and Roy Clover.

You Really Got Me

The Kinks:
featuring an interview with Dave Davies

The Kinks came to town in May 1965 and were hot property having enjoyed two number one singles - 'You Really Got Me' and 'Tired Of Waiting For You'. Not surprisingly the place was packed as Ipswich welcomed a band that was making waves on both sides of the Atlantic thanks to a handful of groundbreaking singles.

Ray and Dave Davies formed the group in 1963 and it wasn't along before they landed a record deal with the Pye label. According to Dave the Ipswich concert was part of their third UK tour. However, not long after their visit to Suffolk he had something of a falling out with the band's drummer Mick Avory. 'Me and Mick had a punch up in Cardiff. He hit me over the head with a cymbal!' Dave and Mick soon patched up their differences and continued on their way to even more chart success including

Left:
The Kinks with two young fans at the Gaumont in 1965.

Above: *The Kinks with adoring fans before their show at the Gaumont in 1965. The Davies brothers along with drummer Mick Avory and bassist Peter Quaife were enjoying yet another hit at the time of their visit. 'Set Me Free' was their fifth hit and there were plenty more to follow. These were heady days for pop fans. The show by The Kinks came only months after visits by The Beatles and The Rolling Stones.*

another chart-topper 'Sunny Afternoon' and the perennial sixties classic 'Dedicated Follower Of Fashion'. Dave has fond memories of the early tours:

The package tours were great. You only had to do about a 15 or 20 minutes if you were headlining. We all used to get into a bus. We didn't have an awful lot of equipment like we do nowadays. It was just like one bus with all the gear stuffed in - a few AC 30s, a harmonica and a couple of guitars. We all used to play cards and have a drink and a chat together. There was a lot of camaraderie, which was really nice. For the most part those package tours were great fun. We got to work alongside people like The Hollies, Gene Pitney and Kim Weston.

Dave's next visit to Ipswich came in 1971 when he and Ray swapped their guitars for football boots. At that time they played soccer matches for charity and both turned out for a Showbiz V1 at Portman Road:

Ray and I love football and we got the chance to play against soccer legends like John Charles and Danny Blanchflower which was amazing. We used to love it. Jess Conrad was the goalie and used to call himself 'The Cat' and we had a great time. The children's TV presenter Brian Cant used to play as well as Tommy Steele and the actor Tony Booth.

At Ipswich the celebrities took on Bobby Robson's Ex-International X1 and although Dave scored twice they were

Right: *The cover of the souvenir programme for a charity match at Portman Road featuring the Davies brothers and other showbiz stars. Personalities from the world of football included the then Ipswich manager Bobby Robson and two former Town bosses Jackie Milburn and Bill McGarry. The game was kicked off by another Portman Road legend - Sir Alf Ramsey.*

Above: *The Showbiz 1V line up in front of the Churchman's stand. Ray Davies is second from the right in the front row. Dave Davies is behind him. Can you spot Ipswich-born children's TV presenter Brian Cant? He's on the far left of the back row.*

THE KINKS

overpowered by the former professionals losing 11-4.

The Kinks were by now very much part of the English music establishment but even though they had a successful start to the 1970s it was a decade beset by problems of both a personal and musical nature. Despite poor record sales and line-up changes the Davies brothers kept the ship afloat and on 25th June 1981 found themselves back at the Gaumont for the 'Better Things' tour. Dave remembers it well:

We had a great time. We had become a rockier band having played American stadium tours. English fans had become very fickle with us at that time. We do have a very odd relationship with our British audience.

Forty years after the release of 'You Really Got Me' interest in the music of The Kinks remains high. It was Dave Davies who came up with that record's scratchy, distorted guitar sound. His big brother Ray may have taken most the plaudits over the years but Dave's considerable input should never be forgotten.

LEFT: *The Kinks still cutting it on stage nearly sixteen years after their first visit to Ipswich.*

Not Fade Away

Rolling Stone and frequent visitor to the Regent Bill Wyman speaks fondly of the Chicago Blues greats

When The Stones rolled into Ipswich in the autumn of 1964 no one was prepared for the mayhem their performances would bring. It was their third visit to the Gaumont in less than a year. Their first appearance towards the end of 1963 had seen them third on a bill which starred The Everly Brothers and Bo Diddley. At that time their only chart hit had been a cover of Chuck Berry's 'Come On' and few could have predicted the impact Mick Jagger, Keith Richards, Charlie Watts, Bill Wyman and Brian Jones would go on to make the following year.

On their second visit to Ipswich they appeared as part of a package show which also included Irish singing trio The Bachelors and Mike 'Come Outside' Sarne. That was in April 1964 and by then 'I Wanna Be Your Man' and 'Not Fade Away' had followed their debut single into the charts. Later that year The Rolling Stones - by now giving The Beatles something to think about - were back in town. Gaumont staff got their first glimpse of the lengths young pop fans would go to just to get close to their idols and it must have been a great relief to theatre manager David Lowe when the show featuring the band's first number one, 'It's All Over Now', was indeed all over.

THE ROLLING STONES

Above: *Young fans surround Mick and Keith at the Gaumont.*

The Rolling Stones, clockwise from top left:

Mick Jagger. Born in Dartford and became friends with Richards at primary school. They lost touch but bumped into each other on a train and discovered their mutual love of the blues. They become one of this country's most successful song-writing partnerships. Jagger was knighted in 2002.

Keith Richards. Also born in Dartford. The perfect foil for Mick Jagger on stage but off stage they have had a love/hate relationship. He has released several solo albums but just like Jagger's solo outings none have come anywhere near the commercial success of the band's releases. Richards wasn't knighted in 2002.

Bill Wyman. Real name William Perks. He joined the band in 1963 after impressing the group with his amplifier at the auditions to replace Dick Taylor. Wyman left The Stones in 1993.

Brian Jones. A founder member of the band. He too played in Blues Incorporated and was a disciple of blues great Elmore James. Jones left The Stones in June 1969. The following month he was found dead in his swimming pool. The coroner recorded a verdict of misadventure, 'drowning while under the influence of alcohol and drugs.'

Charlie Watts. The jazz-loving drummer who lets his playing do the talking. He was very much the quiet member of the group. He came on board at the beginning of 1963 having played alongside Alexis Korner in Blues Incorporated.

Above: *Local teenagers Sylvia Brinkley (left) and Jenni Latham collecting autographs from Mick Jagger, Brian Jones, Keith Richards and Charlie Watts. Lucky fans were able to meet the Stones in a small room under the stage.*

Below: *Stones drummer Charlie Watts (left) and rock guitar legend Keith Richards sign autographs backstage in October 1964.*

Staff at the Gaumont were taken by surprise by fans at the Rolling Stones Show in October 1964. Half-way through the set fans rushed forward and climbed across the orchestra pit and onto the stage. The band played on amid the chaos. From the wings, theatre staff, watched by local police officers, cleared the stage. The fans and the band enjoyed the few minutes of mayhem.

Dave Kindred had been at the theatre to take photographs for the *East Anglian Daily Times*, and *Evening Star*. In the 1960s photography was restricted at the shows. There was a photo call with fans before the show and no photography allowed during the performance.

Dave said, 'As an eighteen year old I had stayed on after taking pictures backstage, to enjoy the show. When the fans leapt on stage I stood on the arms of an empty seat and took these pictures of the fans and the Stones.

'The editor at the *East Anglian* was delighted when reporter Bernard Tubb and I arrived back at the Carr Street office with our "exclusive". Theatre manager David Lowe was less pleased but took the publicity with his usual good humour.'

Sandra Warner from Ipswich saw The Stones support The Everly Brothers, Little Richard and Bo Diddley in 1963:

They were fourth on after Mickie Most. The first half finished with Little Richard. The Ipswich programme had some fascinating facts about the band - Mick Jagger (19) is in his second year at the London School of Economics. Charlie Watts (21) is the Beau Brummel of the group. He has over a hundred pocket-handkerchiefs. Keith Richards (19) worked in a post office and would like to have a house boat on the Thames!

In a souvenir book Sandra bought, costing 2s. 6d (12.5p), Mick Jagger is quoted, 'I give the Stones about another two years.' More than forty years later The Rolling Stones remain one of the most popular live acts in the world. Mick Jagger's expectations have been somewhat exceeded!

Above: *Gaumont manager David Lowe, in formal dress, watches from the stage wing as the fans swarm around The Rolling Stones after crossing the orchestra pit.*

From Buddy to the Beatles

In recent years Rolling Stones bassist Bill Wyman has been a regular visitor to the Regent and he's still packing the place out. These days he fronts The Rhythm Kings, an all star band which has featured the likes of Georgie Fame, Albert Lee, Gary Brooker, Martin Taylor and Mike Sanchez in its ranks. During his sell-out show in January 2004 he quipped that the place hadn't changed a bit since The Rolling Stones took the place by storm forty years earlier.

Bill has made Suffolk his home. He lives at Gedding Hall near Bury St. Edmunds, so Ipswich is very much a local gig for him.

Bill's big musical passion is The Blues. He speaks fondly of Chicago blues greats Muddy Waters and Howlin' Wolf with both of whom he became good friends. The Rolling Stones took their name from a Muddy Waters song and Bill has vivid memories of the band's pilgrimage to Chess Studios in Chicago:

We went there to do some recording in 1964 and when we got to 2120 South Michigan Avenue Muddy helped us in with our gear which shocked us a bit. We watched this icon of ours carrying in our guitars. We got to know him quite well and several years later I got to play bass for him a couple of times at the Montreux Jazz Festival. He always used to say about The Stones - they's my boys! We learned a lot from him and when we did his songs it always said Muddy Waters at the bottom so he got all the money. It helped revive his career.

A few weeks after their most memorable visit to Ipswich The Rolling Stones made it two number ones in a row with their rendition of 'Little Red Rooster', a blues standard penned by another Chicago great Willie Dixon. It was originally recorded by Howlin' Wolf and the following year during another visit Stateside The

Bill Wyman

Stones invited Wolf to perform with them on the American TV show 'Shindig'. Bill says it was the least they could do:

> We idolised the Chicago blues greats and I was lucky enough to have dinner with Wolf. A few years later myself, Eric Clapton and Charlie Watts did 'The London Sessions' album with him.

'Little Red Rooster' was one of many Willie Dixon numbers covered by The Rolling Stones. Born in Vicksburg, Mississippi in 1915, Dixon is the greatest songwriter in the history of the blues and not surprisingly The Rolling Stones loved his work. The other Dixon classics to get their seal of approval were 'I Want To Be Loved', 'I Just Want To Make Love To You', 'Down In The Bottom' and 'Little Baby'. Dixon died in January 1992. Only a few years earlier the big man had picked up a Grammy for his 'Hidden Charms' album - a well deserved accolade for a man who quite rightly declared 'I Am The Blues'.

Above: *Blues great Willie Dixon in conversation with Stephen Foster backstage at the 1990 Chicago Blues Festival. Unfortunately for Stephen, the legendary bassist refused a request to sign his autobiography which Stephen had been reading on the flight over to Windy City. Still, it's not everyday you get to meet a blues giant.*

Move It

Cliff Richard: a regular at the Regent

When the man dubbed 'the Peter Pan of pop' appeared in Ipswich twice in the space in five months in 1959 not even Cliff himself could have imagined the enormous success that was to come his way for the remainder of the century and into the new millennium.

In the early days Cliff was marketed as Britain's answer to Elvis Presley and came in for a lot of stick for his 'too sexy' image on stage. His 1958 debut hit 'Move It' remains one of the finest rock'n'roll records ever made and came close to giving the India-born singer his first UK number one. Cliff didn't have to wait too long to reach the top. In the summer of 1959 'Living Doll' gave him his debut chart-topping single earning him a gold disc. Earlier that year Cliff had delighted his fans in Ipswich and in the coming years the venue was to become a favourite place of his to play. When the Regent re-opened in 1991 he was quick to send a message of support hinting that he might even return one day. His ardent fans would love nothing better than to see him back at the theatre but with Cliff playing stadia and big open air concerts these days his Suffolk faithful realise that's unlikely.

Those lucky enough to have seen the man on stage in the late fifties witnessed the start of a British phenomenon and several decades later pop's pied piper is still calling the tune, as ever, on his own terms. Cliff Richard is a legend in his own lifetime and like many leading figures in pop music has graced the Gaumont stage several times.

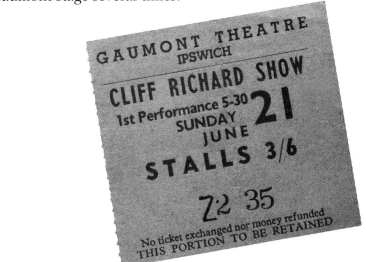

cliff richard

Above:
Cliff presenting Gaumont manager David Lowe with an award.

PROGRAMME

No. 1   FREE TRADE HALL
MANCHESTER
BETTY SMITH and her Quintet
Britain's No. 1 Lady Saxophonist
JOY and DAVE ADAMS
Teenage Favourites
JOHNNY DUNCAN & the Blue Grass Boys
Columbia Recording Stars
MIKE PRESTON
Columbia Recording Star
JIMMY TARBUCK
Your Compere
CLIFF RICHARD & the Drifters

No. 2   PLAZA, BEDFORD
BETTY SMITH and her Quintet
Britain's No. 1 Lady Saxophonist
JOY and DAVE ADAMS
Teenage Favourites
JOHNS and KENNEDY
Two guitars and lots of fun
MIKE PRESTON
Columbia Recording Star
JIMMY TARBUCK
Your Compere
CLIFF RICHARD & the Drifters

No. 3   ODEON, ROMFORD
BETTY SMITH and her Quintet
Britain's No. 1 Lady Saxophonist
JOY and DAVE ADAMS
Teenage Favourites
JOHNS and KENNEDY
Two guitars and lots of fun
MIKE PRESTON
Columbia Recording Star
JOHNNY DUNCAN & the Blue Grass Boys
Columbia Recording Stars
JIMMY TARBUCK
Your Compere
CLIFF RICHARD & the Drifters

No. 4   THE DOME, BRIGHTON
GAUMONT, Ipswich | GAUMONT, Salisbury
THE CHRIS ALLEN RHYTHM GROUP
The well-known Surrey Group appearing at all the principal
Dance Halls in the area
JOY and DAVE ADAMS
Teenage Favourites
MIKE PRESTON
Columbia Recording Star
JOHNNY DUNCAN & the Blue Grass Boys
Columbia Recording Stars
JOHNS and KENNEDY
Two guitars and lots of fun
JIMMY TARBUCK
Your Compere
CLIFF RICHARD & the Drifters

THIS PROGRAMME IS SUBJECT TO ALTERATION AT THE DISCRETION OF THE MANAGEMENT

66

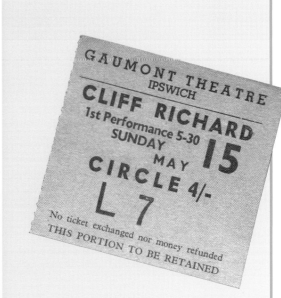

Above:

The young ones meeting the Peter Pan of pop.

Right:

Cliff and the Shadows in the mid 1960s (from the left) Bruce Welch, Brian Bennett, Cliff Richard, John Rostill and Hank Marvin.

Above:

Cliff with more of his adoring young fans.
Also pictured is Johnny Duncan.

CLIFF'S BRITISH CHART-TOPPERS

Living Doll
Travellin' Light
Please Don't Tease
I Love You
The Young Ones
The Next Time/Bachelor Boy
Summer Holiday
The Minute You're Gone
Congratulations
We Don't Talk Anymore
Living Doll (with The Young Ones)
Mistletoe and Wine
Saviour's Day
The Millennium Prayer

ARTHUR HOWES

in association with LESLIE GRADE

presents

THE CLIFF RICHARD SHOW

Souvenir Programme

A Hard Day's Night

Beatlemania comes to Ipswich, October 1964

Forty years on and it's still the most talked about concert in Ipswich's history. On 31st October 1964 The Beatles made a return visit to the Gaumont. The 'Fab Four' had been to town the previous year on their third package tour in as many months. That was on 22nd May 1963 and they'd just notched up their first number one, 'From Me To You'. American singer Roy Orbison was to have headlined that tour but as Beatlemania began to take hold The Big 'O' was forced to do a swap knowing that he couldn't possibly follow The Beatles. It was quite a bill with Gerry and the Pacemakers also in the line-up. We've reproduced the souvenir programme for that night on pages 77 to 92.

The next year Beatlemania swept the nation and by the time John, Paul, George and Ringo returned to the Gaumont they had already become the most successful pop act of all time. Early in 1964 they conquered America and when they returned to the UK they made their first feature film 'A Hard Day's Night'. In the summer of that year Gaumont manager David Lowe took a call from a promoter's secretary:

She said, 'David I've got a date for you, it's very special'. I said, 'it must be something outstanding'. She said, 'it is. It's The Beatles.' Once I'd taken the news in I rang up the Ipswich Borough Chief Constable, James Crawford, to break the news to him. He replied, 'Oh God help us!'

Above: *Beatles fans outside the Gaumont queuing for the hottest tickets in town.*

As you might expect there was a huge demand for tickets and when they went on sale in July. It was like a military operation. Queues went all the way up St. Helens Street and the other way round the back of Botwoods until they met in Woodbridge Road. It was a Sunday morning in July and David Lowe remembers having to get up early to supervise the sale of tickets:

It was 5am. I went to the police control room at the Town Hall and spoke to the officer in charge. We took a walk round the queue and just as we got to the front of the theatre one of the lads on the steps put on 'A Hard Day's Night'. I moved along the queue and I sensed someone staring at me. Most people were asleep but this bloke was looking at me murder. He said, 'Mr Lowe, those tickets had better be there'! A couple of girls had been queuing for seventy-two-hours. They wanted front stall seats and that's just what they got. All tickets had gone by the middle of the afternoon.

Above:
Yes! Roll on Halloween!

Right:
Tonight's the night. The waiting is nearly over.

THE BEATLES

Above:
Competition winners receive a signed guitar from their heroes in the inner foyer.

Right:
A dream come true for one Beatles fan in their tiny dressing room at the Gaumont.

Left:

The Beatles being interviewed before the show by an Anglia TV presenter..

On the night of the concert The Beatles were late getting to the venue. A reporter came up to David Lowe and told him, 'I don't think they are coming. I think this is another of your cheap publicity stunts. I never did believe The Beatles would come to Ipswich.' A few minutes later David took great delight to introducing the reporter to each member of The Beatles. The reporter's face must have been quite a picture.

With dozens of police officers on duty there was very tight security surrounding The Beatles. When they eventually arrived it was in a police van with parking bollards in the back. They'd transferred to that vehicle at Copdock on the outskirts of Ipswich and once they arrived at the Gaumont they were smuggled in through a side exit.

PC Dave Foster was one of the police officers on duty inside the auditorium and come show time the atmosphere was electric:

> *I had to stand with my back to the stage facing the audience. Dozens of screaming girls tried to get to the stage and at times it was quite frightening with so many people pushing towards us. One or two girls fainted and didn't get to see the show at all. I didn't see much of it either although I did glance over my shoulder now and again so I could say I saw The Beatles!*

The Beatles played two shows but very nearly didn't re-appear for the second one. Towards the end of their first performance John Lennon threw his harmonica to the side of the stage. David Lowe's eleven-year-old son Malcolm was at the side of the stage and picked it up. He then took it home with him. John was furious when he

The Beatles signing autographs and keeping young fans amused before their 1963 show in Ipswich.

found out someone had taken his harmonica and made it clear that if he didn't get it back The Beatles wouldn't go back on. David Lowe was alerted and immediately phoned home. By that time Malcolm was fast asleep with John's harmonica under his pillow. A taxi was called to get the instrument back to its rightful owner and just made it back in time for the second performance.

Once the concert was over, the Gaumont staff had to get The Beatles out of the building. With hundreds of fans gathered by the back stage door waiting to get autographs, the Fab Four left via the main entrance. What a memorable moment for the very few people who witnessed The Beatles leaving the building!

Above:

John, Paul, George, Ringo and David. The ultimate photo opportunity. Gaumont manager David Lowe in his office with the greatest pop group of all time. A member of David's staff took the photograph before the 1964 concert.

The Beatles

The Beatles

Roy Orbison

Toppling 'The Big O'. The programme from May 1963
that saw the fab four replace Roy Orbison as top of the bill.

Peter Walsh & Kennedy St. Enterprises
in association with Tito Burns present

THE BEATLES
ROY ORBISON

David Macbeth

Louise Cordet

Erkey Grant

Ian Crawford

Tony Marsh

Terry Young Six

and

GERRY and the
PACEMAKERS

THE BEATLES

JOHN, PAUL AND GEORGE met at school in 1956 and have remained together ever since. They have played as a group with numerous names, various drummers and other augmentations. Their present drummer, Ringo Starr, has only recently joined the group but they have admired and known him since their schooldays.

Back in '56 they, in common with their contemporaries, were on a skiffle kick, washboard, banjo, and the like. For four years they continued in varying forms to entertain in Liverpool clubs, pubs, church halls, and at fêtes. They played for a time at a strip club in the heart of Liverpool's Chinatown.

During this period John left his school to study at the College of Art. During a vacation he worked for five weeks on a building site—with his earnings he bought his first electrified guitar. Paul was at school and attained five subjects in G.C.E. and then English Literature at advanced level. He speaks Spanish and German. George left his school to become an apprentice electrician. But from the beginning there was little doubt that to be successful making music and entertaining was the only goal for these three characters. They form essentially a vocal group but at the same time they comprise musicians of the first order. John plays rhythm guitar, George, lead, and Paul, bass.

Early in 1960 the group was selected at an audition to back Johnny Gentle on a tour of Scotland. This was rough and hard stuff but it led to a beginning. Back in Liverpool they were offered a contract to play in Germany at a night club in Hamburg. At that stage once and for all they left their schools and jobs to accept the offer. In Hamburg they played many hours for few marks,

but their music became formed and their sound was different.

Returning home in December 1960, they opened as the Beatles at a surburban town hall. The reception was rapturous—from there they went from strength to strength playing locally night after night. In April 1961, they were invited to play again in Hamburg at another club offering better conditions.

1962 was an exciting and important year for the Beatles, they spread their wings and their appearances in many different parts of the country always effecting the same result . . . an invitation to return. They have broadcast many times and made numerous appearances on television.

Both sides of their first single were written by Paul and John. "Love me Do" was written in 1958 (in the skiffle days) and "P.S. I love You" was written while the group was playing in Germany. Their second record, "Please, Please Me" reached the No. 1 slot in the Top Thirty, and now "From Me to You" has hit the jackpot again for them.

Gerry Marsden was born in Liverpool on 24th September 1942. He plays lead guitar and handles the solo vocals. He's a prolific song-writer and a keen self-taught instrumentalist. Gerry is pint-sized with a power-packed personality.

The Pacemakers comprise of Freddy Marsden, who was born in Liverpool on 23rd October, 1940. He plays drums and sings. Freddy worked with his younger brother Gerry for six years— in skiffle and rock groups before The Pacemakers were formed in 1959. Les Maguire was born in Wallasey on 27th December 1941. He plays piano and sings. Les joined the group in May 1961.

The youngest member of the group is Les Chadwick who was born in Liverpool on 11th May 1943. He joined Gerry and Freddy in 1959 and has collaborated with Gerry to write more than two dozen original new songs.

GERRY and the PACEMAKERS

Your programme

Terry Young Six   RECORDING GROUP

Ian Crawford   VERSATILE SINGING STAR

Tony Marsh   YOUR COMPERE FOR TONIGHT

Louise Cordet   LOVELY FILM & RECORD STAR

David Macbeth   THE POPULAR VOCALIST

GERRY AND THE PACEMAKERS
HIT RECORDERS OF "HOW DO YOU DO IT"

for tonight

INTERVAL

Terry Young Six TO ENTERTAIN YOU AGAIN

Erkey Grant A REALLY SENSATIONAL ACT

ROY ORBISON FROM THE UNITED STATES

THE BEATLES THE HIT PARADE STARS

God Save the Queen

Programme subject to alteration at the management's discretion

Roy Orbison's dad—an oil driller—has spent most of his life searching for black gold in the oilfields of Texas. Roy, however, who was once a geology student, made his strike at an early age in the recording studios of Nashville, Tennessee when he gave up the oil rigger's drill for a guitar pick.

Roy, now 25, grew up in the oil town in Wink, Texas (population 1500). When his dad wasn't drilling for oil, he was playing guitar and he taught Roy how to play when the boy was 6 years old. When Roy was barely in his teens, he was leading "The Wink Westerners" and conducting a radio show over KVWC in Vernon,

Texas. Roy's first big production, at the ripe old age of sixteen was when he represented the great talent of the Lone Star State (Texas) at the International Lions Convention in Chicago.

Roy Orbison then entered North Texas State College, where he was a geology major. When a fellow student named Pat Boone had his first record success with "Two Hearts", Roy became convinced that he really wanted to search for gold records instead of black gold.

In April, 1956, Roy signed a record contract, and cut his first disc. In 1958, he wrote a song titled "Claudette". The result was another hit record for the Everly Brothers—and a song-writer's contract for Roy.

A prolific song writer, Roy Orbison has had his songs recorded by such artists as : The Everly Brothers, Buddy Knox, Jerry Lee Lewis and the late Buddy Holly. A terrific performer and stylist, his own records are constantly in the national record charts.

Roy's " Crying " and " Candy Man " astounded the music critics with their meteoric rise in the national music charts. This release, a two-sided hit, was the sixth and seventh consecutive Orbison disc to have gone all the way in only twenty months ! In addition to the million-seller "Only the Lonely ", Orbison's past sales breakers include—"Uptown", " Blue Angel"," I'm Hurtin' ", and " Running Scared".

Roy now resides near Nashville in a spacious split-level home on Old Hickory Lake, where his leisure time is spent. When time is available after personal appearances, club dates, recording sessions and the endless chores of song-writing, Roy relaxes by fishing and piloting his high-powered speedboat - one of the fastest on Old Hickory Lake.

ROY ORBISON

LOUISE CORDET

It all started last year in Italy. Louise was holidaying there with her brother Max 18 and her mother Helene Cordet. Evenings, the family would go onto the beach with their Italian friends, and strum guitars and sing the hours away in the soft Italian moonlight. Came Christmas in London and the Cordets decided to cut a private LP of their " beach songs", and send copies to their Italian friends as Christmas gifts. The LP completed, Helene Cordet visited a record producer on her way from the studios. He asked her about the LP she was carrying, and before you could say " Hit Record " her daughter Louise Cordet was under contract.

Louise Cordet was born on February 8th, 1946, in Wraysbury, near Windsor. Her father was a Free French Pilot, She has Greek, French, American and Italian blood. Louise can speak French, English and Italian, and is currently learning Greek. She was educated for five years at the French Lycee in Kensington, is at the moment attending a Convent in Switzerland. She has dark brown eyes, brown hair and is 5ft. 6ins. tall.

Since " I'm just a baby", which was a big success in the charts, Louise has gone from strength to strength with great success in her big tour of France with Johnny Halliday and her very popular new E.P.

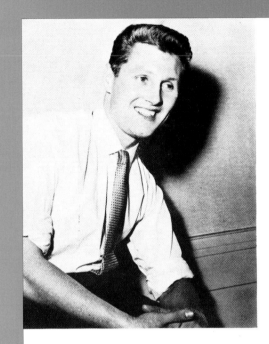

DAVID MACBETH

In November, 1959, David Macbeth—a handsome, husky six-footer from Newcastle-on-Tyne—burst on to the pop music scene via a big selling Top Twenty hit in the shape of "Mr. Blue". Since then, he's enjoyed continued success in the many diverse fields of the entertainment industry —TV, radio, recordings, variety and concerts— and now ranks as one of Britain's busiest vocal stylists.

Quiet, unassuming David Macbeth is overloaded with the kind of talent that makes for lasting stardom. But he's in no immediate hurry to get to the top. He's spent the past two years readying himself for the big break that will eventually come his way, and when stardom beckons, he'll have a wealth of experience behind him to ensure that the opportunity doesn't slip by.

IAN
CRAWFORD

Round the world in 80 songs would describe the short, but exciting, career to date of this young London born singer who emigrated to Australia four years ago. He appeared on television there 300 times and had 5 records in the top ten. After his successes in Australia Ian moved on to America playing television and cabaret dates in Hollywood, Las Vegas, San Francisco and New York.

Ian returned to England via Germany early this year and his first disc to be released is "Everlovin' Me".

ERKEY
GRANT

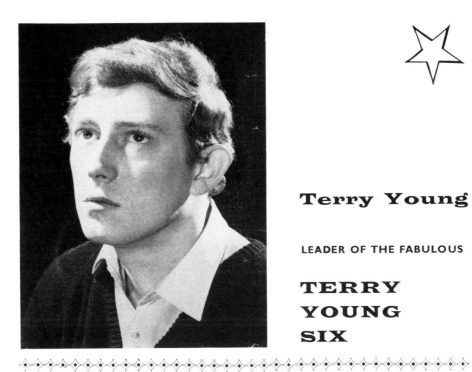

Terry Young

LEADER OF THE FABULOUS

TERRY YOUNG SIX

MEET YOUR COMPERE
FOR TONIGHT

TONY MARSH

1. All gangways passages and staircases must be kept entirely free from chairs or any other obstruction, and no person shall be allowed to sit or stand during any performance or entertainment in such gangways, passages or staircases. 2. The public shall be permitted to leave by all exit and entrance doors after each performance or entertainment. 3. No smoking shall be permitted to take place on the stage except as part of a performance or entertainment. 4. The fireproof safety curtain to the proscenium opening must be lowered and raised at least once during every performance or entertainment, to ensure its being kept in proper working order.

ROY ORBISON

FALLING
c/w Distant drums
HLU 9727   7" single   *(available May 24th)*

ROY ORBISON
Uptown; Paper boy;
Pretty one; With the bug
Ⓜ REU 1354   7" EP   *(new this month)*

CRYIN'
Cryin; The great pretender; Love hurts; She wears my
ring; Wedding day; Summersong; Dance; Lana;
Loneliness; Let's make a memory; Nite life;
Running scared
Ⓢ SAHU 6229   Ⓜ HAU 2437   12" LP

LONELY AND BLUE
Only the lonely; Bye, bye, love; Cry; Blue Avenue;
I can't stop lovin' you; Come back to me; Blue
angel; Raindrops; A legend in my time; I'm hurtin';
Twenty-two days; I'll say it's my fault
Ⓜ HAU 2342   12" LP

STEREO OR MONO RECORDS

LONDON RECORDS division of
THE DECCA RECORD COMPANY LIMITED
DECCA HOUSE   ALBERT EMBANKMENT   LONDON   SE1

This programme was designed and printed by the Hastings Printing Company, Portland Place, Hastings, Sussex. Telephone 2450

Another person with vivid memories of the night Ipswich will always cherish is John Sertic. He recalls John Lennon singing 'Give me money, that's what I want'. It seems the Ipswich audience took this a bit too literally: *I'm an American and was stationed at Bentwaters from 1963 to 1967. A good friend and I attended the Beatles concert at the Gaumont. The thing I remember was the screaming from the girls and the people were throwing those big English pennies at the stage. I have forgotten the other performers but I do remember the song 'My Guy', sung by Mary Wells.*

Right:
Sandra Warner of Ipswich with her programme from the Beatles show in 1964. She remembers sitting in the stalls. Her seat cost 15 shillings (75p).

The Beatles' 1964 British tour took in 27 venues around the UK in only 32 days. For each concert the group played two shows and were paid £850 a night. They played an identical set throughout the tour. These are the songs they performed – 'Twist And Shout', 'Money', 'Can't Buy Me Love', 'Things We Said Today', 'I'm Happy Just To Dance With You', 'I Should Have Known Better', 'If I Fell', 'I Wanna Be Your Man', 'A Hard Day's Night' and 'Long Tall Sally'. The support acts included Motown singing star Mary Wells and Sounds Incorporated. The compère for the show was comedian Bob Bain

94

Left:

Meet the gang now the boys are here. The Beatles enjoying some light refreshment in David Lowe's office.

David Kindred was born in Ipswich in August 1946. He was a pupil of Cliff Lane Junior and Landseer Secondary schools. He joined the *East Anglian Daily Times* Company as a photographer in April 1963. He was soon taking pictures at the Gaumont Theatre of touring bands, including The Everly Brothers, The Byrds, The Beatles and Little Richard.

David took many of the pictures in this book. When the audience leapt onto the stage at The Gaumont during the Rolling Stones show in October 1964 eighteen-year old David was on hand to record the scene.

From The Beatles and Stones, to the local line up of Nick and the Nomads David was there with his camera.

He ended a forty-year career in local news photography as picture editor of the *Evening Star* in January 2004.

David lives in Ipswich and is married to Anne. They have one son, James.

Stephen Foster was born in Ipswich in October 1959. He attended Sidegate Lane Primary and Copleston Secondary schools. After a few years as an insurance claims clerk he landed a job as a trainee reporter at Radio Orwell. In 1990 he joined BBC Radio Suffolk where he has produced and presented a wide range of music and current affairs programmes.

Over the years he has interviewed hundreds of big names including many of the stars featured in this book, among them Sir Cliff Richard, Lonnie Donegan, Bill Wyman, Gene Pitney, Helen Shapiro, Joe Brown and Dave Davies.

In 1995 Stephen worked at Abbey Road studios in London on a special project for EMI Records. He researched and compiled a 5 CD boxed set of recordings by rhythm and blues band Dr Feelgood and that led to extensive work for the group's own label, Grand Records.

Stephen lives in Ipswich and is married to Belinda. They have two sons, Oliver and Joseph.

For a free full catalogue of our books, videos and DVDs please contact:
Old Pond Publishing, Dencora Business Centre, 36 White House Road, Ipswich IP1 5LT, United Kingdom

Phone: 01473 238200 • Fax: 01473 238201
Email: Enquiries@oldpond.com

Website with secure online ordering:
www.oldpond.com